Guildtown Primary School
Perthshire

KU-337-094

00261

261

Space Explorer

THE PLANETS

Patricia Whitehouse

young Explorer

www.heinemann.co.uk/library
Visit our website to find out more information about *Heinemann Library* books.

To order:

 Phone 44 (0)1865 888066

Send a fax to 44 (0)1865 314091

 Visit the Heinemann Bookshop at **www.heinemann.co.uk/library** to browse our catalogue and order online.

First published in Great Britain by Heinemann Library, Halley Court, Jordan Hill, Oxford OX2 8EJ, part of Harcourt Education. Heinemann is a registered trademark of Harcourt Education Ltd.

© Harcourt Education Ltd 2004.
The moral right of the proprietor has been asserted.

All rights reserved. No part of this publication may be reproduced, stored in a retrieval system, or transmitted in any form or by any means, electronic, mechanical, photocopying, recording, or otherwise without either the prior written permission of the Publishers or a licence permitting restricted copying in the United Kingdom issued by the Copyright Licensing Agency Ltd, 90 Tottenham Court Road, London WIT 4LP (www.cla.co.uk).

Editorial: Jilly Attwood and Kate Bellamy
Design: Ron Kamen and Paul Davies
Picture Research: Ruth Blair and Sally Claxton
Illustrator: Jeff Edwards
Production: Séverine Ribierre
Originated by Dot Gradations Ltd
Printed and bound in China by South China Printing Company

The paper used to print this book comes from sustainable resources.

ISBN 0 431 11344 0
08 07 06 05 04
10 9 8 7 6 5 4 3 2 1

British Library Cataloguing in Publication Data
Whitehouse, Patricia
The Planets – (Space Explorer)
523.4
A full catalogue record for this book is available from the British Library.

Acknowledgements
The Publishers are grateful to the following for permission to reproduce photographs: Corbis p. **15** (royalty free); ESA p. **14** (Freie Universitat Berlin); Francisco Diego p. **4**; Hardlines p. **20**; Joe Lawrence p. **5**; NASA p. **17**; Photodisc pp. **10**, **12**, **16**, **18**, **19**, **21**, **24**, **28**; Science Photo Library pp. **8**, **29**; Science Photo Library pp. **9**, **23**, **25** (Mark Garlick), **11**, **13**, **22** (NASA), **26**, **27** (Space Telescope Science Institute/NASA)

Cover photo reproduced with permission of Science Photo Library/NASA

Our thanks to Stuart Clark for his assistance in the preparation of this book.

Every effort has been made to contact copyright holders of any material reproduced in this book. Any omissions will be rectified in subsequent printings if notice is given to the Publishers.

Disclaimer
All the Internet addresses (URLs) given in this book were valid at the time of going to press. However, due to the dynamic nature of the Internet, some addresses may have changed, or sites may have ceased to exist since publication. While the Author and Publishers regret any inconvenience this may cause readers, no responsibility for any such changes can be excepted by either the Author or the Publishers.

Contents

Words written in bold, **like this,** are explained in the Glossary.

 Find out more about space at www.heinemannexplore.co.uk.

Planets are huge objects in space. They are shaped like a ball. Planets are made of rock, metal, ice or **gases**. Almost all planets move around a star.

The Moon, and the planets Venus, Jupiter and Saturn can all be seen from Earth on a clear night.

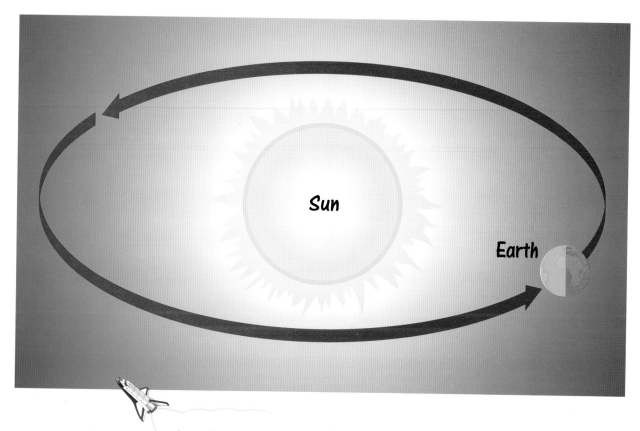

It takes one year for the Earth to move once around the Sun.

Earth is a planet. The Earth is a ball made mostly of rock and metal. It moves around the star we call the Sun.

The Solar System

Our Solar System is made up of the Sun, the planets and their moons. There are nine planets in our Solar System. Earth is one of the planets.

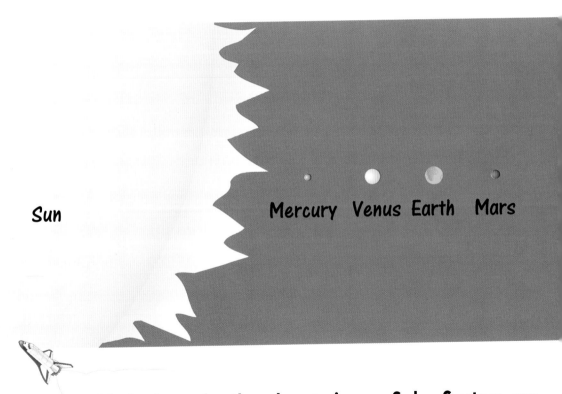

Sun

Mercury Venus Earth Mars

This is the order the planets in our Solar System are usually in. Earth is the third planet from the Sun.

Each planet in the Solar System has its own path, called an **orbit**, around the Sun. The planets are alike in some ways and different in others.

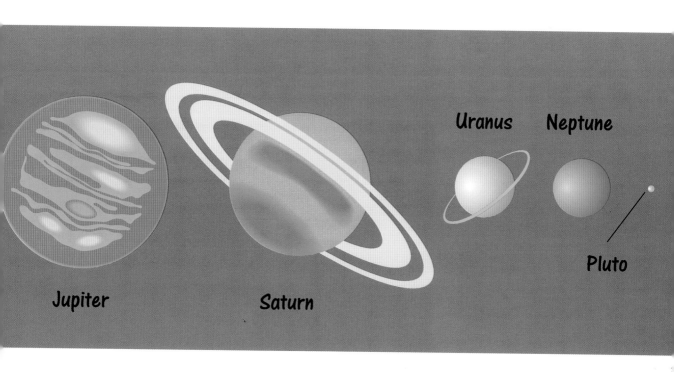

Jupiter

Saturn

Uranus

Neptune

Pluto

Inner planets and outer planets

The four planets closest to the Sun are called the **inner planets**. They are small planets made mostly of rock. They have few or no moons.

Earth is one of the inner planets. The others are Mercury, Venus and Mars.

The five planets furthest away from the Sun are called the **outer planets**. Four of these outer planets are big and made mostly of **gases** so they are called the gas giants.

The four gas giants are Jupiter, Saturn, Uranus and Neptune.

Mercury

Mercury's **orbit** is closest to the Sun. It is the second smallest planet in the Solar System. Mercury has no moons.

Space probes send photographs of Mercury back to Earth.

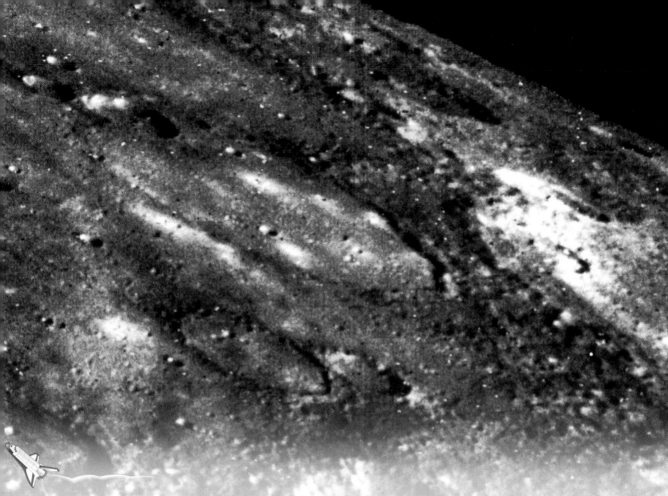

Mercury is covered in holes called craters.

Mercury does not have an **atmosphere**. The sunny side of Mercury heats up to 460°C. That's hot enough to melt a tin pan. Mercury's dark side is about 600°C cooler!

Venus

Venus is the second planet from the Sun. It is sometimes called Earth's twin because both planets are about the same size. Unlike Earth, Venus has no moons.

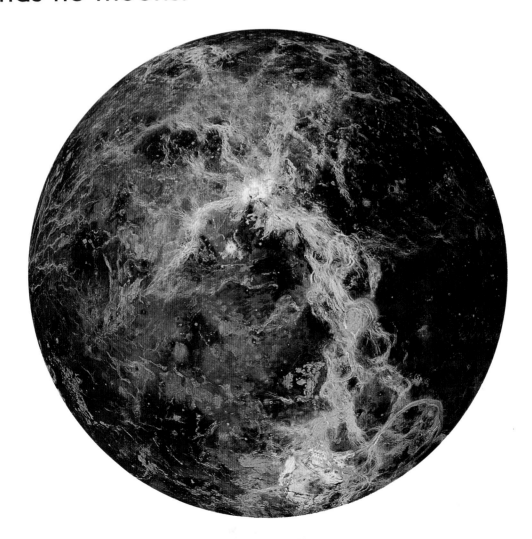

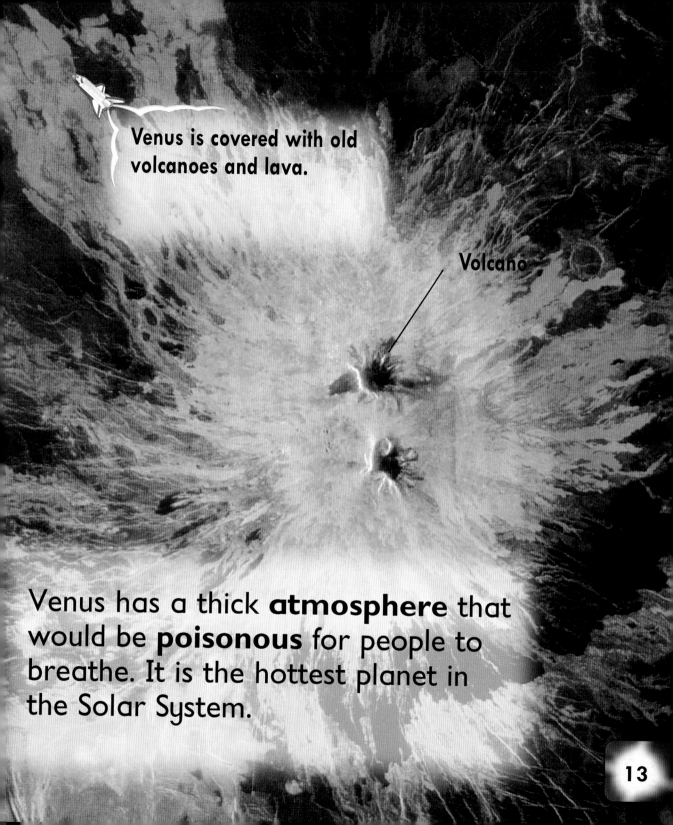

Venus is covered with old volcanoes and lava.

Volcano

Venus has a thick **atmosphere** that would be **poisonous** for people to breathe. It is the hottest planet in the Solar System.

Earth is the third planet from the Sun, and the fifth biggest. It has only one moon.

Earth

Moon

The Earth and its moon as seen from space.

Earth is probably the only planet in the Solar System that has life on it. It has an **atmosphere** we can breathe and there is water.

Living things may not live on any other planet in the Solar System.

Mars

Mars is the fourth planet from the Sun. It is the seventh biggest. It has two potato-shaped moons, named Phobos and Deimos.

Mars is sometimes called the red planet because of its dusty red **surface**. Ice has been found at Mars' north and south poles.

A **space probe** called Mars Pathfinder landed on Mars and sent pictures like this one back to Earth.

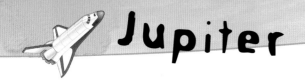

Jupiter

Jupiter is the fifth planet from the Sun. It's the largest planet in the Solar System. It is so large that all the other planets could fit inside of it! Jupiter has at least 60 moons.

Jupiter is the nearest of the gas giants. A giant storm on its **surface** is known as the Great Red Spot. The storm has lasted for over 300 years.

Great Red Spot

The sixth planet from the Sun is Saturn. It's the second largest planet and is one of the gas giants. It has over 30 moons. One of its moons, called Titan, is bigger than the planet Mercury.

Around Saturn is a band of rings made
of rocks and ice. The rings are almost
300,000 kilometres wide, but less than
1 kilometre thick.

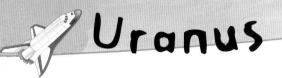

Uranus

Uranus is the seventh planet from the Sun and the third largest. It has at least 21 moons and a dark, thin band of rings.

This picture of Uranus is made up of lots of photos put together, which is why its rings can not be seen.

Uranus is a cold gas giant. It spins on its side. Scientists think a huge **asteroid** hit Uranus and pushed it into its unusual spin.

Uranus looks blue-green because of a gas found in its **atmosphere**.

23

Neptune

Neptune is usually the eighth planet from the Sun. It is about the same size as Uranus. It has at least 11 moons. You need a **telescope** to see Neptune from Earth.

Neptune is made mostly of **gases** and has faint rings like Uranus. Storms sometimes appear as dark spots on its **surface**.

Great Dark Spot

One storm, called the Great Dark Spot, was as big as our Earth.

Pluto

Pluto is usually the ninth planet from the Sun. Part of its **orbit** is inside Neptune's so sometimes it is the eighth planet from the Sun.

Pluto is the smallest planet in the Solar System, and has one moon.

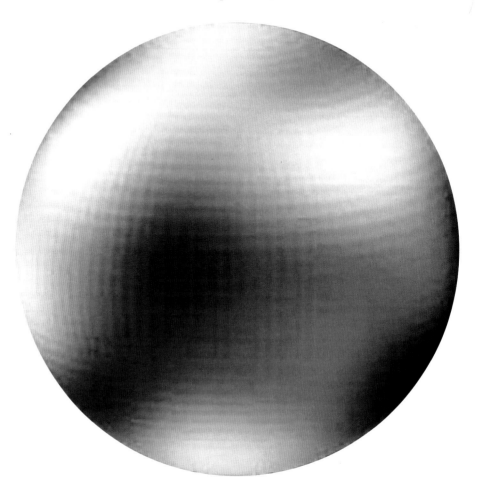

Unlike the other **outer planets**, Pluto is made of a mix of ice and rock. Scientists don't know much about Pluto because it is so far from Earth.

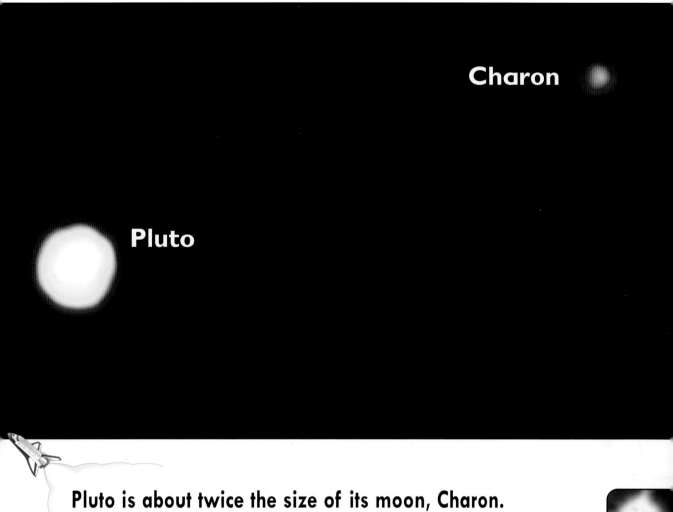

Charon

Pluto

Pluto is about twice the size of its moon, Charon.

Other planets

Astronomers have found other objects at the edges of our Solar System. Some of these objects seem similar to our planets but they are too small to be called planets.

Astronomers use telescopes in space to help them look for other planets.

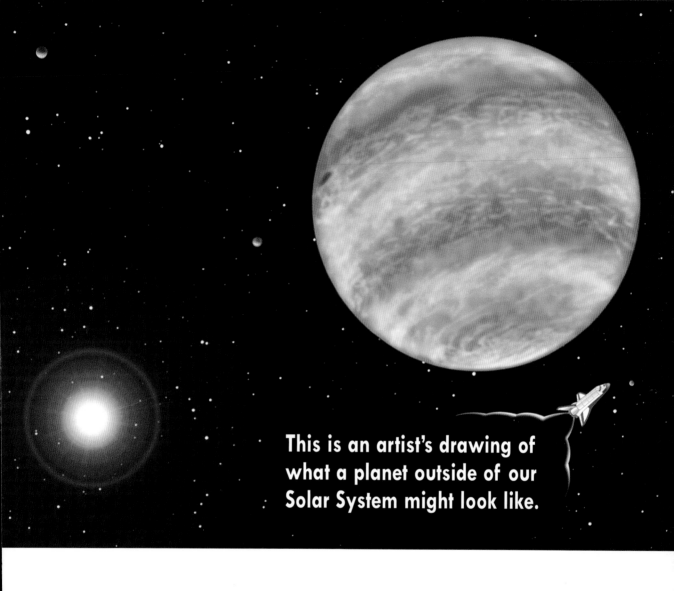

This is an artist's drawing of what a planet outside of our Solar System might look like.

Using new telescopes, astronomers have found over 100 planets outside our Solar System. Could they have life on them? Astronomers in the future may find out.

Amazing planet facts

The temperature on Venus can reach 484°C, which is hot enough to melt lead.

Winds on Neptune can reach 1000 kilometre per hour.

In 2004, scientists found what could be the tenth planet in our Solar System. They have called it Sedna.

Some scientists think that that there are diamonds in the centre of Uranus.

Find out more about space at www.heinemannexplore.co.uk.

Glossary

asteroid large rock that orbits the Sun

astronomers scientists who study space

atmosphere layer of gases around a planet

gas air-like material that is not solid or liquid

inner planets four planets closest to the Sun

orbit the path one object makes around another

outer planets five planets past the inner planets

poisonous harmful

space probe a spacecraft that sends information back to Earth about space

surface the top or outside of an object

telescope an instrument used to make far-away objects look bigger

More books and websites

The Sun (Space Explorer), Patricia Whitehouse (Heinemann Library, 2004)
The Earth (Space Explorer), Patricia Whitehouse (Heinemann Library, 2004)

www.esa.int
www.nasa.gov/audience/forkids

Index

Titles in the *Space Explorer* series include:

Hardback   0 431 11347 5

Hardback   0 431 11348 3

Hardback   0 431 11345 9

Hardback   0 431 11342 4

Hardback   0 431 11341 6

Hardback   0 431 11344 0

Hardback   0 431 11343 2

Hardback   0 431 11340 8

Hardback   0 431 11346 7

Find out about the other titles in this series on our website www.heinemann.co.uk/library